## 30 DAYS *of* NOURISHMENT FOR YOUR SPIRIT AND SOUL

**LORNA BARNABY-ROBINSON**

## 30 DAYS *of* NOURISHMENT FOR YOUR SPIRIT AND SOUL

*For my uncle, Winston Barnaby, and everyone who passed away from COVID-19. You are truly missed.*

*Copyright © 2021 by Lorna Barnaby-Robinson*

*All rights reserved. Except permitted under the U.S. Copyright Act of 1976, no part of this publication may be used, reproduced, distributed or transmitted by in any form or by any means, graphic, electronic or mechanical or stored in a database or retrieval system, without the prior written permission to the publisher except in the case of brief quotations embodied in critical articles and reviews.*

*Scripture quotations marked (AMP) are taken from the Amplified Bible, Copyright © 1954, 1958, 1962, 1964, 1965, 1987 by The Lockman Foundation. Used by permission.*

*Unless otherwise indicated, Scriptures are taken from the Holy Bible, New International Version®, NIV® Copyright © 1973, 1978, 1984, 2011 by Biblica, Inc.™ Used by permission. All rights reserved worldwide.*

*Scripture quotations marked MSG are from The Message. Copyright © Eugene H. Peterson 1993, 1994, 1995, 1996, 2000, 2001, 2002 by Tyndale House Foundation. Used by permission of Tyndale House Publishers, Inc., Carol Stream, Illinois 60188. All rights reserved.*

*Scriptures quotations marked NKJV are from the New King James Version. Copyright © 1979, 1980, 1982, Thomas Nelson, Inc., Publishers. All rights reserved. Used by permission.*

*Scripture quotations marked (NLT) are taken from the Holy Bible, New Living Translation, copyright ©1996, 2004, 2015 by Tyndale House Foundation. Used by permission of Tyndale House Publishers, Carol Stream, Illinois 60188. All rights reserved.*

*Scripture quotations marked NRSV are from the Revised Standard Version of the Bible, copyright © 1946, 1952, and 1971 National Council of the Churches of Christ in the United States of America. Used by permission. All rights reserved worldwide.*

*Vine Publishing's name and logo are trademarks of Vine Publishing, Inc.*

*ISBN: 978-1-7367483-0-5 (paperback)*
*ISBN: 978-1-7367483-2-9 (e-book)*

*Library of Congress Cataloging-in-Publication Data*
*Library of Congress Control Number: 2021915340*

*Published by Vine Publishing, Inc.*
*New York, NY*
*www.vinepublish.com*

*Printed in the United States of America*

# CONTENTS

| | |
|---|---|
| DAY 1 | A Divine Release |
| DAY 2 | It Won't Break You |
| DAY 3 | Freedom To Be |
| DAY 4 | Rest In His Peace |
| DAY 5 | Hope Again |
| DAY 6 | Trusting In Divine Faithfulness |
| DAY 7 | Divine Healer |
| DAY 8 | The Battle Has Already Been Won |
| DAY 9 | Free Indeed |
| DAY 10 | No More Poison |
| DAY 11 | Walking In Humility |
| DAY 12 | Stay Joyful |
| DAY 13 | The Blessings Is Yours |
| DAY 14 | God Sees |
| DAY 15 | Delayed But Not Denied |

# CONTENTS CON'T.

| | |
|---|---|
| DAY 16 | It's Sufficient |
| DAY 17 | Strength For The Day |
| DAY 18 | It's The Little Things |
| DAY 19 | Choose Wisely |
| DAY 20 | Clearing Your Path |
| DAY 21 | The Doctor Is In |
| DAY 22 | The Gift of A New Day |
| DAY 23 | A Bright Future |
| DAY 24 | Be Revived |
| DAY 25 | Never Alone |
| DAY 26 | Thriving Not Surviving |
| DAY 27 | Your Next Level |
| DAY 28 | Wait On Me |
| DAY 29 | What Will He Find |
| DAY 30 | Courage To Win |

# INTRODUCTION

I've often asked myself what life would be like if God had not introduced himself to me. I have wondered what life would be like without God's infinite love through his son, Jesus Christ. Every day I have the chance to experience God's grace and mercy. Each day I awake to a new revelation of His goodness, but I also recognize that each day I must do my part to remain spiritually-filled and nourished.

It is so easy to get caught up in the day-to-day life activities and forget to feed our souls. Much like the necessity for life-giving, nutritionally-good food to maintain a healthy body, we need the life-giving, nutritionally-good Word of God to maintain a healthy spirit and soul.

*Spiritual Food on The Go* was written to provide spiritual nourishment rooted in God's Word. It was written to provide spiritual sustenance that refreshes and revitalizes the soul. I wrote it for busy individuals who are always on the go. I wrote it for those who may feel spiritually dry and empty. I wrote it for those who are in need of strength—strength for the day; strength to make it through the difficulties of life; strength to keep going.

In this devotional you will find quick spiritual nuggets that enrich, strengthen and uplift. It is my hope that as you take these quick bites, your faith will grow, and you will find yourself drawing closer and closer to God. You may not have an hour to spare but as you travel to work, or as you sit at your desk, or as you take a break between chores, meetings or classes, take five minutes to ingest these spiritual goodness. As you partake of this *Spiritual Food on The Go*, it is my prayer that you will be encouraged and renewed. It is my prayer that you will find just what you need to keep going another day. God loves you and I celebrate you. Now, let's eat!

"I am the *BREAD* of life; whoever comes to me shall not hunger, and whoever believes in me shall never thirst."

-JESUS (JOHN 6:35 ESV)

# A DIVINE RELEASE

God's plan for creation is for us to have fellowship and relationship with Him. It was God who walked with Adam in the garden of Eden. It is God's desire to walk with you, talk with you and be present in every aspect of your life. Today, you may feel as if no one is there for you. You may be feeling lonely, but God is by your side. He is that friend who never leaves you or forsakes you. He is that friend whom you can lean on, confide in and bring all your cares to. Today, He says, "Cast all your cares upon me, for I care for you" (1 Peter 5:7). What anxieties do you have to cast upon Him? What concerns are bothering you? What burdens are you carrying? Today it is my hope that you will cast it, throw it, and release it to the Lord in prayer.

# DAY 1

Casting all your cares [all your anxieties, all your worries, and all your concerns, once and for all] on Him, for He cares about you [with deepest affection, and watches over you very carefully]. *(1 PETER 5:7 AMP)*

**Write a short prayer or reflection here.**

# IT WON'T BREAK YOU

Sometimes it feels as if we are facing one issue after another. Sometimes it seems as if the struggles are overbearing. Sometimes it feels as if we are about to break. But today, God wants you to know that His strength is made perfect in your weakness (2 Corinthians 12:9). What does that mean? It means that when you are at your lowest point; when you feel like it's all too much, God will strengthen you under the pressure. Whatever you are struggling with today, it will not break you. You may be experiencing the most difficult season of your life, but God promises to uphold you. You will make it through this. Today, God says, "Fear not, for I am with you."

# DAY 2

Do not fear [anything], for I am with you. Do not be afraid, for I am your God. I will strengthen you, be assured I will help you; I will certainly take hold of you with My righteous right hand [a hand of justice, of power, of victory, of salvation]. *(ISAIAH 41:10 AMP)*

**Write a short prayer or reflection here.**

# FREEDOM TO BE

We all have something that we need to break free from. It may be a bad habit, a bad attitude or it may be the need to break from unforgiveness, shame or a host of other things. Whatever it is that's holding you back and preventing you from living in true freedom, God wants you to know that He is a chain-breaker. You may not have the power to break your own chains, but God will break them when you give it over to Him. Today, I encourage you to give Him the thing that's holding you in bondage. Give Him your pain, your anger, your resentment, your shame, that habit; give Him that secret sin. God wants you to be free to live the life He created you to live. John 8:36 says, "If the son sets you free, you are free indeed." God is willing and is able to set you free.

I will walk about in freedom, for I have sought out your precepts. *(PSALM 119:45 NIV)*

**Write a short prayer or reflection here.**

# REST IN HIS PEACE

Sometimes it's hard to hold on to peace when faced with the trials of life. Sometimes there is an inner turmoil within our hearts. Many of us have sought peace in all the wrong places. We sought peace in money, houses, cars and companionship, only to realize that there was no peace in material gain. True peace comes from knowing that regardless of the situation, God is in control. True peace is found in the unconditional love of God. True peace is in God's faithfulness. Jesus said, "Peace I leave with you; my peace I give you. I do not give to you as the world gives. Do not let your hearts be troubled and do not be afraid" (John 14:27). Today, God is extending His peace to you. Embrace it and rest in it.

# DAY 4

In peace [and with a tranquil heart] I will both lie down and sleep, for You alone, O Lord, make me dwell in safety and confident trust. *(PSALM 4:8 AMP)*

**Write a short prayer or reflection here.**

## HOPE AGAIN

Hope is a confident expectation that what God promised he is able to do. Hope in God gives us the strength to make it through the most trying and difficult times of our lives. Hope is the engine that causes us to press through the hurt, pain and turmoil that life sometimes brings. Hope is what keeps us joyful in the midst of it all. Today, I encourage you to expect God's goodness in your life. Today, I encourage you to believe again, see again, hope again.

Happy are those whose help is the God of Jacob, whose hope is in the Lord their God. *(PSALM 146:5 NKSV)*

**Write a short prayer or reflection here.**

# TRUSTING IN DIVINE FAITHFULNESS

Trust is important for all types of relationships. Trust is the bond that keeps a husband and wife together. Trust is what strengthens the bond between a mother and child. Trust is important, but the fact is, sometimes people will disappoint us. People will break our hearts. People won't always be truthful, but God is not like men and women. We can completely trust in the Lord because of his faithfulness. Numbers 23:19 reminds us that God is not human that he should lie, not a human being, that he should change his mind. Does he speak and then not act? Does he promise and not fulfill? God's promises are in God's Word and whatever he has spoken over your life, He is faithful to bring it to pass. Today, make a renewed decision to trust God.

# DAY 6

> Trust in and rely confidently on the Lord with all your heart and do not rely on your own insight or understanding. *(PROVERBS 3:5 AMP)*

**Write a short prayer or reflection here.**

# DIVINE HEALER

Are you in need of healing? Our God is a divine Healer. Healing is a gift of God's grace and mercy. If you have been praying for healing in your body, mind or soul, know today that the great Physician has heard your cry. There is nothing too hard for our God. Sickness is not too hard. In fact, God says, "See, I am the Lord, the God of all flesh; is anything too hard for me?" (Jeremiah 32:27). Today, ask yourself, "Is there anything too hard for my God?" In spite of any ailment; in spite of what it looks like or feels like, God is able to heal and restore. Keep praying. Keep believing. The divine Healer is able.

# DAY 7

> Heal me, O Lord, and I shall be healed; save me, and I shall be saved, for you are my praise. *(JEREMIAH 17:14 ESV)*

**Write a short prayer or reflection here.**

# THE BATTLE HAS ALREADY BEEN WON

Life does not guarantee that everything will go well or go our way. In fact, Jesus said, "In this world you will have trouble. But take heart! I have overcome the world" (John 16:33 NIV). There will always be trials and tribulations—battles that we have to face, but the good news is that the Lord has already given us the victory. The struggles you are facing will not conquer you. You may feel overwhelmed and it may even look as if you are losing, but today, God wants to remind you that you are an overcomer because of the Cross. Today, I encourage you to give every battle, every struggle, every trial over to the Lord and watch God fight for you. You are victorious.

For the Lord your God is the one who goes with you to fight for you against your enemies to give you victory. *(DEUTERONOMY 20:4 NIV)*

**Write a short prayer or reflection here.**

## FREE INDEED

Have you been going to God in prayer asking to be released from a bad habit, a destructive lifestyle, or even from your pattern of thinking? We all have had to go to God to ask for help to change. If you know that there is something that you are struggling with then, today know that deliverance is possible when you go to God with a humble, repentant heart. God wants you to be free. Free to live for Him; free to live without the bondage of sin; free to live victoriously. Today, make the decision to live free. Submit everything that has been keeping you in bondage to God. He is a chain-breaker.

So if the Son sets you free, you will be free indeed. *(JOHN 8:36 NIV)*

**Write a short prayer or reflection here.**

# NO MORE POISON

Someone once said, "Unforgiveness is like drinking poison and expecting our enemy to die." Unforgiveness is more harmful to the one holding the grudge than it is to the offender. Have you been drinking poison? Have you been holding on to unforgiveness? Today, I encourage you to let it go. Let go of the hurt, the betrayal, the anger, the resentment and harmful everything you have been holding onto. Forgiveness is freedom; it releases to love. Each day we are in need of God's forgiveness, but forgiveness is only guaranteed when we ourselves forgive others. Today, choose to forgive.

# DAY 10

In prayer there is a connection between what God does and what you do. You can't get forgiveness from God, for instance, without also forgiving others. If you refuse to do your part, you cut yourself off from God's part.
*(MATTHEW 6:14-15 MSG)*

**Write a short prayer or reflection here.**

## WALKING IN HUMILITY

Pride has a way of masking itself and may go undetected. It looks like not wanting to ask for directions when lost—that's pride. It looks like the inability to say I am sorry—that's pride. It looks like someone who knows it all—that's pride. But James 4:6 reminds us that "God opposes the proud but shows favor to the humble." A humble spirit is a pleasing spirit to God. If you are struggling with pride, bring it to the Lord in prayer and the power of the Holy Spirit will empower you to live in humility. Today, resist pride and embrace walking humbly.

# DAY 11

> Humble yourselves [with an attitude of repentance and insignificance] in the presence of the Lord, and He will exalt you [He will lift you up, He will give you purpose]."
> *(JAMES 4:10 AMP)*

**Write a short prayer or reflection here.**

## STAY JOYFUL

How can we describe joy? It is a feeling of excitement, pleasure, and contentment. Joy is good for the soul. But, sometimes circumstances of life will try to rob us of that good joyful feeling. Sometimes the events of life aren't always pleasurable. Question: Has something or someone robbed you of your joy? Today, God wants you to know that it is in His presence that you will find the fullness of joy. With tears rolling down your cheeks, get into God's presence and there you will find peace, contentment and joy. Pray, worship and praise—that's where the presence of the Lord resides. Even in the worst situation, in God's presence you will have joy.

You will show me the path of life; In Your presence is fullness of joy; In Your right hand there are pleasures forevermore.

*(PSALM 16:11 AMP)*

**Write a short prayer or reflection here.**

## THE BLESSING IS YOURS

God wants you to be prosperous. Do you believe that? Oftentimes when we think of prosperity, we associate it with financial wealth, success and economic well-being. But prosperity is so much more than financial gain. It is success in all areas of your life. If you are struggling to succeed in any area of your life, then today I encourage you to commit it to God. When you surrender your plans to the Lord, He will give you wisdom, knowledge and understanding to succeed in all that you do. As you give it to God, may He prosper and bless you abundantly.

Commit your works to the Lord [submit and trust them to Him], and your plans will succeed [if you respond to His will and guidance]. *(PROVERBS 16:3 AMP)*

**Write a short prayer or reflection here.**

## GOD SEES

We all face painful situations. Unfortunately, we will have to face the death of a loved one, or the death of a relationship, or just the death of a dream. All these things are painful. Perhaps you are dealing with a painful situation and you are trying to cope. Today, God wants you to know that He is there to bring you through it all. God's arms are open to comfort you. When you are in despair, know that He is right there with you collecting every tear. God is with you and He will never forsake you. Today, give Him your broken heart. Give him your pain and He will give you beauty for ashes (Isaiah 61:3).

He heals the brokenhearted and binds up their wounds [healing their pain and comforting their sorrow]. *(PSALM 147:3 AMP)*

**Write a short prayer or reflection here.**

# DELAYED BUT NOT DENIED

*H*ave you been waiting on God for a long time? Have you been believing God for the answer to a specific request and it seems that there is no answer? Maybe it has been a week, a month, a year or maybe even a few years, and still there is no answer. The reality is that having and maintaining patience is not always easy. But today, God wants to remind you that delay is not denial. Do not give up hope. Do not stop believing. Keep praying. Keep seeking and keep expecting. God does not move on our time, but He is always on time.

Wait for and confidently expect the Lord;
Be strong and let your heart take courage.
Yes, wait for and confidently expect the Lord.
*(PSALM 27:14 AMP)*

**Write a short prayer or reflection here.**

# IT'S SUFFICIENT

Grace is a wonderful gift from God. As you read this, think about the blessing of God's grace. Grace is goodness when we don't even deserve it. Grace is God's abundant love that flows from the Cross and empowers our lives. Today, God says, "When you think you can't make it through, My grace is sufficient to sustain you." God's grace will keep you. Grace will strengthen you. God's grace will empower you to do what you would not be able to do by your own strength and ability. Today, tap into God's grace.

But He has said to me, "My grace is sufficient for you [My lovingkindness and My mercy are more than enough—always available—regardless of the situation]; for [My] power is being perfected [and is completed and shows itself most effectively] in [your] weakness. Therefore, I will all the more gladly boast in my weaknesses, so that the power of Christ [may completely enfold me and] may dwell in me. *(2 CORINTHIANS 12:9 AMP)*

**Write a short prayer or reflection here.**

## STRENGTH FOR THE DAY

The pressure of life—the demands of your job, home and life—can sometimes be stressful. Stress can be mentally and emotionally draining. You may feel as if you don't know whether you are coming or going. You may feel overwhelmed by the circumstances of life. You may feel frustrated and even angry, but today, God wants to remind you that regardless of what you face, His steadfast love abounds and He is faithful to handle all the stressors of life. Today, be encouraged and know that God will help and guide you.

DAY 17

The steadfast love of the Lord never ceases, his mercies never come to an end; they are new every morning; great is your faithfulness.
*(LAMENTATIONS 3:22-23 NRSV)*

**Write a short prayer or reflection here.**

## IT'S THE LITTLE THINGS

*E*very day we have the opportunity to open our eyes, it's a day to say, thank you. It is so easy to forget the little blessings of life. It is so easy to take things and people for granted. It is easy to focus on what we don't have, rather than focusing on what we do have. You may not have everything you want, but if you are reading this, then you have everything you need. You have life. Today, see God in the little things and be thankful for all things. Instead of complaining, choose to be grateful. God has great blessings in store for you. Be thankful.

I will give thanks and praise the Lord, with all my heart; I will tell aloud all Your wonders and marvelous deeds. *(PSALM 9:1 AMP)*

**Write a short prayer or reflection here.**

# CHOOSE WISELY

God is such a loving God that He gives each of us free will. We have the freedom to live a life of faith, or live in fear. We have the freedom to live a life filled with love and forgiveness, or to live in bitterness. We have the freedom to speak life, or to speak death. God gives us free will but it is His desire that we live according to His plan and Word. Today, the question is, are you making choices that are grounded in faith and God's Word, or are you being led by your own will and desires? God's plans are greater than you can ever imagine. Whatever you may be facing, seek God's wisdom and choose God's way.

# DAY 19

For the Lord gives [skillful and godly] wisdom; from His mouth comes knowledge and understanding. *(PROVERBS 2:6 AMP)*

**Write a short prayer or reflection here.**

# CLEARING YOUR PATH

There is nothing you will ever face in life that God hasn't already resolved. Perhaps, you have been trying to figure out how things will turn out. Maybe you can't see the light at the end of a dark tunnel. Maybe you just don't see a clear path. No matter the situation, God wants to remind you that He is your way-maker. He will make a way out of no way. He will shift things in your favor. He will make your paths smooth and clear. He will remove every obstacle and every barrier in your way. Today, hold on to the hands of God and watch Him lead and guide you.

I will go before you and level the mountains; I will shatter the doors of bronze and cut through the bars of iron. *(ISAIAH 45:2 AMP)*

**Write a short prayer or reflection here.**

# THE DOCTOR IS IN

God does not promise us a life without pain and trials. Sometimes we may face the unfathomable. Sometimes we may have to face heartbreak, mental unrest, a bad diagnosis, and other ailments. With life comes its fair share of trials, and sometimes even sickness. But in spite of what ails you, today be encouraged, because the Doctor is in. God is the Divine Physician who heals all our wounds and diseases. Our God is still a miracle-worker. There is nothing impossible or irreversible for God. He can heal your broken heart, settle your mind, and heal your body. Today, be encouraged. Keep praying. Keep trusting, and keep believing.

# DAY 21

The Lord nurses them when they are sick and restores them to health. *(PSALM 41:3 NLT)*

**Write a short prayer or reflection here.**

## THE GIFT OF A NEW DAY

Have you ever wished you could get a "do-over"? Have you ever wished you could start again? The beauty and gift of this day is the ability to start over. God has given you a brand-new day to dream again, to believe again, to let go of the past, and to live again. Forget the disappointments and failures of yesterday. Forget old history. Let go of what's behind you and look forward to what's ahead. Today, see new possibilities, expect God's blessings, and embrace the gift of a new day.

# DAY 22

Forget about what's happened; don't keep going over old history. Be alert, be present. I'm about to do something brand-new. It's bursting out! Don't you see it? There it is! I'm making a road through the desert, rivers in the badlands. *(ISAIAH 43:18-19 MSG)*

**Write a short prayer or reflection here.**

## A BRIGHT FUTURE

Are you going through a trial that seems overwhelming? Are you facing a situation that has you worried or anxious about your future? Sometimes the burdens of life seem unbearable, but no matter what it looks like, God wants to remind you that He has a great plan for your life. Today, be encouraged because your future is secured. The sovereign Lord has already gone before you and has prepared a future filled with love, blessings, hope and prosperity. You may not see it now, but trust God that what's ahead of you is greater than you can ever imagine.

For I know the plans and thoughts that I have for you,' says the Lord, 'plans for peace and well-being and not for disaster, to give you a future and a hope.
*(JEREMIAH 29:11 AMP)*

**Write a short prayer or reflection here.**

# BE REVIVED

Some days getting out of bed isn't easy. Some days, finding the strength to keep going is difficult. Some days we may feel as if we just don't have the energy to keep fighting, keep believing, and keep holding on. But today, God wants to remind you that His Word is your lifeline. God's Word is His promise that never fails. God promises to help you (Isaiah 41:13)—he'll be a very present and well-proved help in trouble (Psalm 46:1). God promises to supply all of your needs (Philippians 4:19). His promise is that you will come out of affliction unharmed (Isaiah 43:2). God's Word is life, peace and hope. Today, God wants to revive you. Let His promises breathe new life, new hope and new possibilities into your situations.

This is my comfort in my affliction, that Your word has revived me and given me life.
*(PSALM 119:50 AMP)*

**Write a short prayer or reflection here.**

# NEVER ALONE

Some days, we may feel as if we are traveling through life by ourselves. Some days, we may feel alone and even lonely. Some days, you may feel as if there is no one to talk with, seek guidance from, comfort you, or to just be there. But in those moments, God wants to remind you that you have the Holy Spirit. He is your best friend with whom you share your deepest thoughts. He is your Comforter who comforts you when you are feeling low. He is your Guide who will lead to God's perfect will. Jesus promised that you will never be alone. He has given you the Helper, the One who enables you, the One who teaches you, the One who reveals God's truths. Today, God wants you to know that even when you feel lonely, you are never alone. The Holy Spirit is always with you.

And I will ask the Father, and He will give you another Helper (Comforter, Advocate, Intercessor—Counselor, Strengthener, Standby), to be with you forever—I will not leave you as orphans [comfortless, bereaved, and helpless]; I will come [back] to you. *(JOHN 14:16,18 AMP)*

**Write a short prayer or reflection here.**

# THRIVING NOT SURVIVING

*H*ave you ever asked yourself, "Am I thriving or am I surviving?" To thrive is to grow, to flourish, and to prosper. But on the other hand, to survive is to simply stay afloat; it is getting by day-by-day. So, are you thriving or surviving? While God is there through your survival stage, God wants you to thrive. God wants you to grow in your faith. He wants you to grow in your love. He wants you to grow in your obedience. He wants you to flourish in your relationship with Him and others. He wants you to prosper in the works of your hands. Today, God is calling you beyond your comfort zone. God is calling you to THRIVE.

> The righteous will flourish like a palm tree.
> They will grow like a cedar of Lebanon.
> *(PSALM 92:12 NIV)*

**Write a short prayer or reflection here.**

## YOUR NEXT LEVEL

It's easy for us to stay content. It's easy for us to remain at a comfortable level. It's easy to stay stagnant with no spiritual growth. Comfortable feels good, but today God wants you to move beyond what feels good and go to the next level. Where do you believe God wants you to go higher? What does going higher look like for you? Today, take the time to ask God what your next level is. Your next level will lead to a stronger, deeper relationship with God. Your next level will lead to spiritual growth and maturity. Your next level will lead to fulfillment and purpose. When you are willing to go higher, you can rest assured that God will equip you for your next level.

# DAY 27

> Therefore let us get past the elementary stage in the teachings about Christ, advancing on to maturity and perfection and spiritual completeness.
> *(HEBREW 6:1 AMP)*

**Write a short prayer or reflection here.**

## WAIT ON ME

*H*aving patience isn't always easy. There are times when we just get tired of waiting. There are times when we want what we want, when we want it. We get impatient with God's response to our prayers. We may not understand why things don't happen when we want them to happen, but today God is reminding you that His timing is perfect. What have you been waiting for? What prayers have not been answered? You may be tempted to make things happen, tempted to rush the process, but today, God says, "Wait on Me." God hears all and sees all. He knows the desires of your heart. When you wait patiently on God's timing, He will exceed your expectations. Wait on the Lord.

Wait for and confidently expect the Lord; be strong and let your heart take courage; yes, wait for and confidently expect the Lord.
*(PSALM 27:14 AMP)*

**Write a short prayer or reflection here.**

## WHAT WILL HE FIND?

What we do on earth matters. How we live our life matters. Our earthly home is our temporary home. We are guaranteed an external existence with God in heaven, but what we do on earth matters. Christ will return at a time when we least expect Him. The question is, how will he find you living? Would He be pleased with what He finds? Are you fully committed to Him, or are you partially devoted? Are you living according to God's Word, God's terms, God's desires for your life, or have you chosen your own path? What will Jesus find on His return? Today, God wants to remind you to be ready for His second coming. Live a life that strives to please Him. Today, God says, "Seek My will and do your part to bring Me glory on earth."

# DAY 29

> Therefore, you [who follow Me] must also be ready; because the Son of Man is coming at an hour when you do not expect Him.
> *(MATTHEW 24:44 AMP)*

**Write a short prayer or reflection here.**

## COURAGE TO WIN

Courage is the ability to push beyond your fears to do something that seems difficult, frightening, or challenging. Courage is the ability to tap into the power that's within you. Like David and Goliath, you may have to face some giants in your life. But today, God is reminding you that with His strength you will be victorious. What do you need courage for today? In God's strength, you can be bold and confident. God will never give you a task that He does not equip and empower you to accomplish. Today God says, "Step out. Move in faith and be courageous." You will win!

But as for you, be strong and do not lose courage, for there is reward for your work.
*(2 CHRONICLES 15:7 AMP)*

**Write a short prayer or reflection here.**

# ABOUT THE AUTHOR

Lorna Barnaby-Robinson is a native of Jamaica, West Indies, and a woman of many talents. A servant of God, her vision is to feed others spiritually as well as physically. Lorna is a certified Chaplain with the New York State Force, a faithful volunteer in her home church, and a culinary chef.

As a Chaplain Mrs. Barnaby-Robinson provides the ministry of presence to souls who are often facing distressing situations. Lorna graduated from Borough of Manhattan Community College with a degree in Human Services and after working for many years with the United Parcel Service, she decided to pursue one of her passions and enroll in classes at the Culinary Tech Center in New York City. She graduated with her culinary arts certificate in 2015 and went on to launch, Lorna's Catering and Sweets.

Throughout the years Lorna not only served with her local church, but she leads devotions for several prayer groups and has been committed to serving other nonprofit organizations. Among her many accomplishments, Lorna is most proud of being a mother of four children, a grandmother to her six grandchildren, and a loving, devoted wife.

www.ingramcontent.com/pod-product-compliance
Lightning Source LLC
Chambersburg PA
CBHW040527120526
44589CB00050B/2792